MAX on life
cd-book :: study

Growing the Marriage of Your Dreams

**4 Interactive Bible Studies
for Individuals or Small Groups**

MAX LUCADO

THOMAS NELSON PUBLISHERS

CONTENTS

HOW TO USE
THIS STUDY GUIDE

Congratulations! You are making God's Word a priority. These moments of reflection will change you forever. Here are a few suggestions for you to get the most out of your individual study.

1

As you begin each study, pray that God will speak to you through his Word.

2

Read the overview to each study, then listen to the audio segment, taking notes on the worksheet provided.

3

Following the audio segment, respond to the personal Bible study and reflection questions. These questions are designed to take you deeper into God's Word and help you focus on God and on the theme of the study.

4

There are three types of questions used in the study. *Observation* questions focus on the basic facts: who, what, when, where, and how. *Interpretation* questions delve into the meaning of the passage. *Application* questions help you get practical: discovering the implications of the text for growing in Christ. These three keys will help you unlock the treasures of Scripture.

5

Write your answers to the questions in the spaces provided or in a personal journal. Writing brings clarity and deeper understanding of yourself and of God's Word.

6

Keep a Bible dictionary handy. Use it to look up any unfamiliar words, names, or places.

7

Have fun! Studying God's Word can bring tremendous rewards to your life. Allow the Holy Spirit to illuminate your mind to the amazing applications each study can have in your daily life. ■

INTRODUCTION

GROWING THE MARRIAGE OF YOUR DREAMS

How is your marriage? Consider it your Testore cello. This finely constructed, seldom seen instrument has reached the category of rare and is fast earning the status of priceless. Few musicians are privileged to play a Testore; even fewer are able to own one.

I happen to know a man who does. He, gulp, loaned it to me for a sermon. Wanting to illustrate the fragile sanctity of marriage, I asked him to place the nearly-three-centuries old instrument on the stage, and I explained its worth to the church.

How do you think I treated the relic? Did I twirl it, flip it, and pluck the strings? No way. The cello is far too valuable for my clumsy fingers. Besides, its owner loaned it to me. I dared not dishonor his treasure.

On your wedding day, God loaned you his work of art: an intricately crafted, precisely formed masterpiece. He entrusted you with a one-of-a-kind creation. Value her. Honor him. Having been blessed with a Testore, why fiddle around with anyone else?

Make your wife the object of your highest devotion. Make your husband the recipient of your deepest passion. Love the one who wears your ring. Succeed at home first to grow the marriage of your dreams. ■

Your home is your giant-size privilege,
your towering priority.

MAX LUCADO

LESSON ONE:

UNDERSTANDING WHAT EVERY WIFE NEEDS

Enjoy life with the wife you love.

ECCLESIASTES 9:9

OVERVIEW

One of my favorite childhood memories is greeting my father as he came home from work. After school, my brother and I would take our positions on the couch and watch cartoons, always keeping one ear alert to the driveway. Even the best "Daffy Duck" would be abandoned when we heard his car.

I can remember running to meet dad and getting swept up in his big (often sweaty) arms. As he carried me toward the house, he'd put his big-brimmed straw hat on my head, and for a moment I'd be a cowboy. We'd sit on the porch as he removed his oily work boots (never allowed in the house). As he took them off I'd pull them on, and for a moment I'd be a wrangler. Then we'd go indoors and open his lunch pail. And leftover snacks, which he always seemed to have, were for my brother and me to split.

It was great. Boots, hat, and snacks. What more could a five-year-old want?

But suppose, for a minute, that is all I got. Suppose my dad, rather than coming home, just sent some things home. Boots for me to play in. A hat for me to wear. Snacks for me to eat.

Would that be enough? Maybe so, but not for long. Soon the gifts would lose their charm. Soon, if not immediately, I'd ask "Where's Dad?"

Or consider something worse. Suppose he called me up and said, "Max, I won't be coming home anymore. But I'll send my boots and hat over, and every afternoon you can play in them."

No deal. That wouldn't work. Even a five-year-old knows it's the person, not the presents, that makes a reunion special. It's not the frills; it's the father.

Your presence is just as important to your wife. No gift has greater value, no present means more. Be present for your wife.

PART 1:
FOLLOW-ALONG NOTES

USE THIS WORKSHEET AS YOU LISTEN TO "GROWING THE MARRIAGE OF YOUR DREAMS, PART 1."

· Peter's Message to Husbands – 1 Peter 3:7

EVERY WIFE NEEDS HER HUSBAND TO PROVIDE

1. Permanence

Husbands should be there _____ and _____.

Women hunger for _____.

2. Perception

Men and women are different.

A woman's intuition is _____.

3. Protection

Correct definition of weaker vessel_____.

4. Praise

Your wife needs to feel _____.

PART 2:
GOING DEEPER

PERSONAL STUDY AND REFLECTION

- Describe the "work of art" that God gave you on your wedding day. Make it a point to share those feelings with your wife.

_____

_____

_____

_____

_____

_____

· List ways you currently seek to show love to your wife. Then, list areas where you need to improve in expressing love to your wife.

_____

_____

_____

_____

_____

_____

_____

· *Be present. Be there. Let her question many things, but never let her question the fact that you are going to be there.*

· Reflect on the meaning of permanence in your home.

_____

_____

_____

_____

· Give a plan of action to solidify your presence for your family.

_____

_____

_____

_____

· Looking back on your youth, what incorrect perceptions of relationships
  did you bring into your marriage? What positive changes have taken place
  in the marriage over the years?

_____

_____

_____

_____

· Be _____ with the _____ you married when

  you were _____, she gives you _____, . . . she is as

  _____ and graceful as a deer. Let her _____ always

  make you happy; let her love always hold you _____.

  Proverbs 5:18-19

- *One of the roles that men have in the family is to provide a sense of safety, a sense of protection, and a sense of security.*

- Share ways you provide protection for your family.

_____

_____

_____

_____

_____

_____

_____

_____

- *Husbands, your wife needs to feel significant. So much of what she does is hidden from view. We men need to praise our wives.*

- List some qualities of your wife that you need to praise.

_____

_____

_____

_____

_____

_____

_____

_____

What is there in the vale of life
half so delightful as a wife
when friendship, love, and peace combine
to stamp the marriage-bond divine?

WILLIAM COWPER

LESSON TWO:

UNDERSTANDING WHAT EVERY HUSBAND NEEDS

But each one of you must love
his wife as he loves himself,
and a wife must respect her husband.

EPHESIANS 5:33

OVERVIEW

Have you ever considered the impact that excess baggage has on relationships? We've made this point at our church by virtue of a drama. A wedding is reenacted in which we hear the thoughts of the bride and groom. The groom enters, laden with luggage. A bag dangles from every appendage. And each bag is labeled: guilt, anger, arrogance, insecurities. This fellow is loaded. As he stands at the altar, the audience hears him thinking, *Finally, a woman who will help me carry all my burdens. She's so strong, so stable, so . . .*

As his thoughts continue, hers begin. She enters, wearing a wedding gown but, like her fiancé, covered with luggage. Pulling a hanging bag, shouldering a carry-on, hauling a makeup kit, paper sack—everything you could imagine and everything labeled. She has her own bags: prejudice, loneliness, disappointments. And her expectations? Listen to what she is thinking: *Just a few more minutes and I've got me a man. No more counselors. No more group sessions. So long, discouragement and worry. I won't be seeing you anymore. He's going to fix me.*

Finally they stand at the altar, lost in a mountain of luggage. They smile their way through the ceremony, but when given the invitation to kiss each other, they can't. How do you embrace someone if your arms are full of bags?

For the sake of those you love, learn to set them down.

And, for the sake of the God you serve, do the same. He wants to use you, you know.

God has a great race for you to run. Under his care you will go where you've never been and serve in ways you've never dreamed. But you have to drop some stuff. How can you share grace if you are full of guilt? How can you offer comfort if you are disheartened? How can you lift someone else's load if your arms are full with your own?

For the sake of those you love, travel light.

For the sake of the God you serve, travel light.

For the sake of your own joy, travel light.

There are certain weights in life you simply cannot carry. Your Lord is asking you to set them down and trust him.

PART 1:
FOLLOW-ALONG NOTES

USE THIS WORKSHEET AS YOU LISTEN TO "GROWING THE MARRIAGE OF YOUR DREAMS, PART 2."

EVERY HUSBAND IS STRENGTHENED WHEN A WIFE

· Encourages him – give him your praise

A man has two mirrors in his life: _____

_____

Proverbs 21:9

Proverbs 19:13

Proverbs 21:19

Two ways to encourage your husband:

Value _____

Affirm _____

- Empowers him – make him your priority
  Genesis 2:18
  Exodus 18:4
  Psalm 121:1-2

  The role of a helper - Titus 2:4,5

- Endears him – guard your appearance for him
  Song of Solomon 2:2

- Entices him – grant your affection to him
  Proverbs 5:15,20

- Inspires him – nourish your own faith
  Proverbs 31:30

PART 2:
GOING DEEPER

PERSONAL STUDY AND REFLECTION

- Based on Max's teaching, which of your husband's needs do you succeed at providing? Which need work?

_____

_____

_____

_____

_____

- *A man desperately needs the affirmation of his wife. The secret longing of a man is to hear his wife say, "I respect you."*

· Think back to the male influences in your life. What character traits did you most admire?

_____

_____

_____

_____

· **Read Proverbs 31:10-31.** List ways to become the type of wife listed in these verses.

_____

_____

_____

_____

· What misconceptions did you bring into the marriage? How did you overcome them? Are there any still needing work?

_____

_____

_____

_____

· Share some ways to improve your relationship with your husband based on things you need to change about yourself.

_____

_____

_____

_____

- List any baggage that you brought into the marriage that needs to be put down and left for God to handle.

_____

_____

_____

_____

_____

_____

_____

- *The role of a wife with her husband is a divine role, a high and holy call. You are never more like God than when you are encouraging your husband.* ■

Many persons have the wrong idea
of what constitutes true happiness.
It is not attained through self-gratification,
but through fidelity to a worthy purpose.

HELEN KELLER

LESSON THREE:

BUILDING THE RIGHT FENCES

God has joined the two together,
so no one should separate them.

MATTHEW 19:6

OVERVIEW

David succeeded everywhere except for home. And if you don't succeed at home, do you succeed at all? How do we explain David's disastrous home? How do we explain David's silence when it comes to his family? No psalms written about his children or wife. He never talked about them.

Aside from the prayer he offered for Bathsheba's baby, Scripture gives no indication that he ever prayed for his family. He prayed about the Philistines, interceded for his warriors. He offered prayers for Jonathan, his friend, and for Saul, his archrival. But as far as his family is concerned, it's as if they never existed.

Was David too busy to notice them? Maybe. He had a city to settle and a kingdom to build.

Was he too important to care for them? "Let the wife raise the kids; I'll lead the nation."

Was he too guilty to shepherd them? After all, how could David, who had seduced Bathsheba and intoxicated and murdered Uriah, correct his sons when they raped and murdered?

Too busy. Too important. Too guilty. And now? Too late. A dozen exits too late. But it's not too late for you. You home is your giant-size privilege, your towering priority. Do not make David's tragic mistake.

David missed the sanctity of marriage. He collected wives as trophies. He saw spouses as a means to his pleasure, not a part of God's plan. Don't make his mistake. Be fiercely loyal to one spouse. *Fiercely* loyal. Don't even look twice at someone else. No flirting. No teasing. No loitering at her desk or lingering in his office. Who cares if you come across as rude or a prude? You've made a promise. Keep it. Your spouse is not your trophy but your treasure.

PART 1:
FOLLOW-ALONG NOTES

USE THIS WORKSHEET AS YOU LISTEN TO "GROWING THE MARRIAGE OF YOUR DREAMS, PART 3."

· Genesis 39:1-9

TEMPTATIONS JOSEPH FACED

_____

_____

_____

_____

_____

We are more _____ in times of prosperity.

P R I N C I P L E S   O F   L O Y A L T Y

1. Have a conviction before the _____.

   Genesis 39:8

2. Recognize that love involves _____.

   Genesis 39:9

3. Have sense to avoid the _____.

   Genesis 39:10

   Romans 13:14

4. Stay shocked by _____.

   Proverbs 5:3-4

5. Retreat is better than _____.

   Genesis 39:12

PART 2:
GOING DEEPER

PERSONAL STUDY AND REFLECTION

- Compare the temptations faced by David and Joseph in the Old Testament. Now compare each of the responses to that temptation. What lessons can you take away from both situations?

_____

_____

_____

_____

_____

_____

- *The media has led you to believe that adultery is a common event. There is a message that comes to you on a regular basis through the media that would have you to believe that everyone is doing it.*

- Describe a plan of action to build the right fences in your marriage.

_____

_____

_____

_____

_____

_____

_____

· Give a personal definition of showing loyalty in marriage.

_____

_____

_____

_____

_____

_____

_____

· And God said, so a _____ will _____ his father and

mother and be _____ with his _____, and the two will

become _____ _____. Matthew 19:5

- Think back to your wedding vows. What vow do you feel has been easy to keep? What vow has been difficult to keep?

_____

_____

_____

_____

_____

_____

_____

_____

- List sources of strength and support in your life to help in the battle to protect your marriage.

_____

_____

_____

_____

- As you read the following Scriptures, summarize the lesson obtained from each that will help in protecting your marriage.

Proverbs 6:25 _____

Psalm 119:37 _____

Job 31:1 _____

1 John 2:16 _____

Proverbs 5:3-23 _____

Proverbs 14:7-9 _____

Proverbs 17:24 _____

Hebrews 4:13 _____

Ecclesiastes 2:10 _____

Proverbs 6:24-35 _____

Proverbs 7:5-27 _____

Ecclesiastes 11:9 _____

Proverbs 3:7 _____

Proverbs 11:2-6 _____

Proverbs 27:12 _____

Proverbs 31:30 _____

*A successful marriage is an edifice
that must be rebuilt every day.*

ANDRE MAUROIS

LESSON FOUR:

SEX: GOD'S GOOD GIFT

Those who live in love live in God,
and God lives in them.

1 JOHN 4:16

OVERVIEW

Be quick to understand, God is not antisex. Dismiss any notion that God is anti-affection and anti-intercourse. After all, he developed the whole package. Sex was his idea. From his perspective, sex is nothing short of holy.

He views sexual intimacy the way I view our family Bible. Passed down from my father's side, the volume is one hundred years old and twelve inches thick. Replete with lithographs, scribblings, and a family tree, it is in my estimation, beyond value. Hence, I use it carefully.

When I need stepstool, I don't reach for the Bible. When we need old paper for wrapping, we don't rip a sheet out of this book. We reserve the heirloom for special times and keep it in a chosen place.

Regard sex the same way—as a holy gift to be opened in a special place at special times. The special place is marriage, and the time is with your spouse.

Sex apart from God's plan wounds the soul. Sex according to God's plan nourishes the soul. Consider his plan. Two children of God make a covenant with each other. They disable the ejection seats. They fall into each other's arms beneath the canopy of God's blessing, encircled by the tall fence of fidelity. Both know the other will stay even as skin wrinkles and vigor fades. Each gives the other exclusive for-your-eyes-only privileges.

Gone is the guilt. Gone the undisciplined lust. What remains is a celebration of permanence, a tender moment in which the body continues what the mind and the soul have already begun. A time in which "the man and his wife were both naked and were not ashamed" (Genesis 2:25).

Such sex honors God. And such sex satisfies God's children.

PART 1:
FOLLOW-ALONG NOTES

USE THIS WORKSHEET AS YOU LISTEN TO "GROWING THE MARRIAGE OF YOUR DREAMS, PART 4."

· Genesis 2:24-25

Healthy intimacy _____ a marriage.

Pure sex develops _____.

FOUR REASONS GOD CREATED SEX

1. Marital sex _____ the marriage covenant.

   Genesis 2:24

2. Marital sex _____ mutual trust.

   Genesis 2:25

3. Marital sex _____ healthy pleasure.

Genesis 26:8

4. Marital sex _____ the earth.

Genesis 1:28

• Sex is a celebration of permanence, a tender moment in which the body continues what the mind and the soul have already begun.

PART 2:
GOING DEEPER

PERSONAL STUDY AND REFLECTION

· Share some of the warped views of sex the world throws at us.

_____

_____

_____

_____

_____

_____

_____

- *The marriage bed helps husband and wife stitch their souls together. Sexuality in God's plan is a good idea.*

- As you read Genesis 2:24-25, how do you view God's plan for husband and wife?

_____

_____

_____

_____

_____

_____

_____

_____

- Contrast God's plan with the plan of society today. Contrast the results of following each plan.

_____

_____

_____

_____

_____

_____

_____

_____

_____

· Give reasons pure sex in a marriage strengthens the relationship.

_____

_____

_____

_____

_____

_____

_____

_____

· *Sexual activity in the right realm cements a relationship permitting the husband and wife to do physically what they are already doing emotionally.*

- Write a covenant to your spouse to follow God's plan of marital sex.

I pledge _____

_____

I commit to _____

_____

I promise _____

_____

I vow to _____

_____

I will always _____

_____ ■

PROMISES FROM GROWING THE MARRIAGE OF YOUR DREAMS

Savor the following promises that God gives to those who determine to have the marriage of their dreams. One way that you can carry the message of this study with you everywhere in your heart is through the lost art of Scripture memorization. Select a few of the verses below to commit to memory.

Be happy with the wife you married when you were young.
She gives you joy, as your fountain gives you water.
She is as lovely and graceful as a deer.
Let her love always make you happy;
let her love always hold you captive.

PROVERBS 5:18-19

The wife does not have full rights over her own body;
her husband shares them.
And the husband does not have full rights over his own body;
his wife shares them.

1 CORINTHIANS 7:4

It is hard to find a good wife,
because she is worth more than rubies.
Her husband trusts her completely.
With her, he has everything he needs.
She does him good and not harm for as long as she lives.

PROVERBS 31:10-12

But each one of you must love his wife as he loves himself,
and a wife must respect her husband.

EPHESIANS 5:33

When a man finds a wife, he finds something good.
It shows that the LORD is pleased with him.

PROVERBS 18:22

Enjoy life with the wife you love.

ECCLESIASTES 9:9

Marriage should be honored by everyone,
and husband and wife should keep their marriage pure.
God will judge as guilty those who take part in sexual sins.

HEBREWS 13:4

Wives, yield to the authority of your husbands,
because this is the right thing to do in the Lord.
Husbands, love your wives and be gentle with them.

COLOSSIANS 3:18-19

Be an example to the believers with your words,
your actions, your love, your faith, and your pure life.

1 TIMOTHY 4:12

It is not fancy hair, gold jewelry, or fine clothes that should make you beautiful.
No, your beauty should come from within you—the beauty of a gentle
and quiet spirit that will never be destroyed and is very precious to God.
In this same way the holy women who lived long ago
and followed God made themselves beautiful,
yielding to their own husbands.

1 PETER 3:4-5

God made husbands and wives to become one body and one spirit
for his purpose—so they would have children who are true to God.
So be careful, and do not break your promise to the wife
you married when you were young.

MALACHI 2:15

The husband should give his wife all that he owes her as his wife.
And the wife should give her husband all that she owes him as her husband.

1 Corinthians 7:3

A wise wife is a gift from the LORD.

Proverbs 19:14

Do not let those evil people lead you away by the wrong they do.
Be careful so you will not fall from your strong faith.

2 Peter 3:17

As the church yields to Christ, so you wives should yield to your husbands in
everything. Husbands, love your wives as Christ loved he church and gave himself
for it.

Ephesians 5:24-25

Don't share in the sins of others. Keep yourself pure.

1 Timothy 5:22

In the same way, you husbands should live with your wives in an understanding
way, since they are weaker than you. But show them respect, because God gives
them the same blessing he gives you—the grace that gives true life.

1 Peter 3:7

SUGGESTIONS FOR MEMBERS OF A GROUP STUDY

The Bible says that we should not forsake the assembling of ourselves together (see Hebrews 10:25). A small-group Bible study is one of the best ways to grow in your faith. As you meet together with other people, you will discover new truths about God's Word and challenge one another to greater levels of faith. The following are suggestions for you to get the most out of a small-group study of this material.

1. Come to the study prepared. Follow the suggestions for individual study mentioned previously. You will find that careful preparation will greatly enrich your time spent in group discussion.

2. Be willing to participate in the discussion. The leader of your group will not be lecturing. Instead, he or she will be encouraging the members of the group to discuss what they have learned. The leader will be asking the questions that are found in this guide.

3. Stick to the topic being discussed.

4. Be sensitive to the other members of the group. Listen attentively when they describe what they have learned. You may be surprised by their insights! Many questions do not have "right" answers, particularly questions that aim at meaning or application. Instead the questions push us to explore the passage more thoroughly.

5. When possible, link what you say to the comments of others. Also be affirming whenever you can. This will encourage some of the more hesitant members of the group to participate.

6. Expect God to teach you through the passage being discussed and through the other members of the group. Pray that you will have an enjoyable and profitable time together, but also that as a result of this study, you will find ways that you can take action individually and/or as a group.

7. Remember that anything said in the group is considered confidential and should not be discussed outside the group unless specific permission is given to do so.

LEADER'S GUIDE

LESSON ONE:

UNDERSTANDING WHAT EVERY WIFE NEEDS

1. Begin the session with prayer. Ask God to be with you as you begin to study his Word together.

2. Play the audio segment of the CD entitled "Growing the Marriage of Your Dreams, Part 1." Encourage group members to take notes in the section of their study guide entitled "Follow-Along Notes."

3. Begin group discussion by asking the following questions. Allow each group member ample time to answer, if they desire to do so.

   - Describe the differences in men and women that you have observed.

   - List qualities you admire in godly women.

   - How does misunderstanding your spouse compound problems of everyday life?

   - Share some of the insights you learned from other female family members whether it be your mother, sister, cousin or aunt.

- How can you value you wife in practical ways?

4. Remind everyone to complete the "Going Deeper: Personal Study and Reflection" section for lesson two before the next group session.

5. Be sure to close in prayer. Invite the group participants to share prayer requests with the group and encourage them to pray for one another.

LESSON TWO:
UNDERSTANDING WHAT EVERY HUSBAND NEEDS

1. Begin the session with prayer. Ask God to be with you as you begin to study his Word together.

2. Play the audio segment of the CD entitled "Growing the Marriage of Your Dreams, Part 2." Encourage group members to take notes in the section of their study guide entitled "Follow-Along Notes."

3. Begin group discussion by asking the following questions. Allow each group member ample time to answer, if they desire to do so.

- Share ways you affirm your husband.

- List the attributes of your husband that you value.

- Read Titus 2:4-5. Describe in your own words the role of a helper.

- Men need the respect of their wife. Give examples of showing that respect.

- How do you show respect for your husband's version of manhood?

4. Remind everyone to complete the "Going Deeper: Personal Study and Reflection" section for lesson three before the next group session.

5. Be sure to close in prayer. Invite the group participants to share prayer requests with the group and encourage them to pray for one another.

LESSON THREE: BUILDING THE RIGHT FENCES

1. Begin the session with prayer. Ask God to be with you as you begin to study his Word together.

2. Play the audio segment of the CD entitled "Growing the Marriage of Your Dreams, Part 3." Encourage group members to take notes in the section of their study guide entitled "Follow-Along Notes."

3. Begin group discussion by asking the following questions. Allow each group member ample time to answer, if they desire to do so.

   • Share your opinion of the action of Joseph in his time of temptation.

   • Give excuses the world gives to justify adultery.

   • Who is hurt when the marriage vows are broken? Does it reach beyond the husband and wife?

   • Give practical steps to take in building fences to protect your marriage.

   • Memorization of Scripture can be a very useful tool in fighting temptation. Share some verses that you find helpful for this particular subject.

4. Remind everyone to complete the "Going Deeper: Personal Study and Reflection" section for lesson four before the next group session.

5. Be sure to close in prayer. Invite the group participants to share prayer requests with the group and encourage them to pray for one another.

LESSON FOUR: SEX: GOD'S GOOD GIFT

1. Begin the session with prayer. Ask God to be with you as you begin to study his Word together.

2. Play the audio segment of the CD entitled "Growing the Marriage of Your Dreams, Part 4." Encourage group members to take notes in the section of their study guide entitled "Follow-Along Notes."

3. Begin group discussion by asking the following questions. Allow each group member ample time to answer, if they desire to do so.

   • How do you protect yourself from adopting the world's view of sex?

   • Share the positive aspects of God's plan for sex.

   • Explain how sex outside of marriage wounds the soul.

   • What can the church do to better educate people to the fact that sex is part of God's plan?

4. Be sure to close in prayer. Invite the group participants to share prayer requests with the group and encourage them to pray for one another.

MAX LUCADO'S
MAX on life
S E R I E S

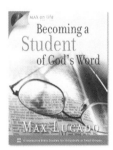

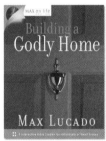

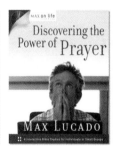

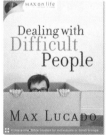

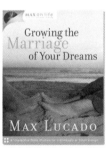

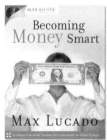

AVAILABLE WHEREVER BOOKS ARE SOLD.